books by
BOXER

www.booksbyboxer.com

Published by
Books By Boxer, Leeds, LS13 4BS UK
Books by Boxer (EU), Dublin D02 P593 IRELAND
© Books By Boxer 2022
All Rights Reserved
MADE IN CHINA
ISBN: 9781909732988

Knock Knock...
Who's there?
Yoda Lady
Yoda Lady who?
I didn't know you could yodel!

Knock Knock...
who's there?
Tally
Tally who?
No, Tally-ho!

Knock Knock...
who's there?
A broken pencil
A broken pencil who?
Never mind... it's pointless.

Knock Knock...
Who's there?
Daisy
Daisy who?
Daisy me rollin, they hatin'.

Knock Knock...
who's there?
Olive
Olive who?
Olive you too!

Knock Knock...
who's there?
Luke
Luke who?
**Luke through the keyhole
and find out!**

Knock Knock...
Who's there?
Owls
Owls who?
Yeah, they do!

Knock Knock...
Who's there?
Cash
Cash who?
No thanks, I'll stick to the peanuts.

Knock Knock...
Who's there?
Dejav
Dejav who?
Knock Knock...

Knock Knock...
who's there?
A wood wok
A wood wok who?
**A wood wok 500 miles,
and a wood wok 500 more!**

Knock Knock...
Who's there?
Spell
Spell who?
Ok, fine. W-H-O.

Knock Knock...
Who's there?
Ida
Ida who?
Surely it's pronounced Idaho?

Knock Knock...
who's there?
To
To who?
No, it's pronounced to WHOM.

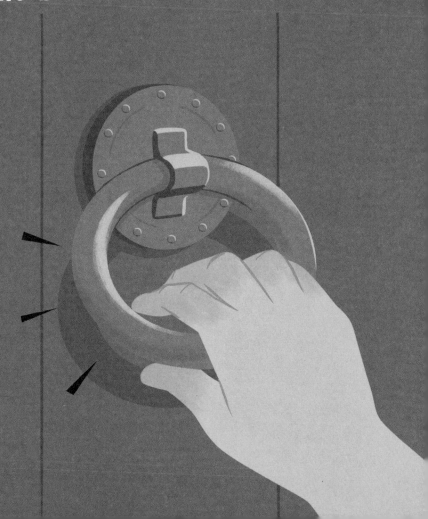

Knock Knock...
Who's there?
Wa
Wa who?
What are you so excited about?

Knock Knock...
who's there?
Ice cream soda
Ice cream soda who?
Ice cream soda people can hear me!

Knock Knock...
who's there?
Haven
Haven who?
Haven you heard enough of
these knock knock jokes?

Knock Knock...
Who's there?
Adore
Adore who?
**Adore is between us,
please open up!**

Knock Knock...
Who's there?
Alex
Alex who?
Alex-plain when you open the door!

Knock Knock...
who's there?
Cargo
Cargo who?
Cargo beep beep!

Knock Knock...
who's there?
Ya
Ya who?
No, I use Google.

Knock Knock...
who's there?
Art
Art who?
R2D2!

Knock Knock...
Who's there?
Moustache
Moustache who?
**I moustache you a question, but
I'll shave it for later!**

Knock Knock...
who's there?
Peng
Peng who?
Peng-who-in!

Knock Knock...
Who's there?
Chell
Chell who?
I have my violin, let's play!

Knock Knock...
Who's there?
Figs
Figs who?
Figs the doorbell, it's broken!

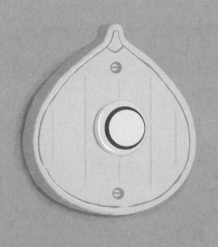

Knock Knock...
Who's there?
Dishes
Dishes who?
Dishes the police, open up!

Knock Knock...
Who's there?
Kanga
Kanga who?
Actually, it's Kangaroo!

Reedturn to Sender
address unknown

Knock Knock...
who's there?
Reed
Reed who?
**Reedturn to sender,
address unknown.**

Knock Knock...
Who's there?
Tat
Tat who?
I think you should get an anchor!

Knock Knock...
who's there?
Stopwatch
Stopwatch who?
**Stopwatch you're doing
and let me in!**

Knock Knock...
Who's there?
Can
Can who?
**I'd rather take
a ferry!**

Knock Knock...
Who's there?
Isabel
Isabel who?
Isabel working? I had to knock!

Knock Knock...
Who's there?
Amos
Amos who?
A mosquito. Bzzz!

Knock Knock...
Who's there?
Oink Oink
Oink Oink who?
Are you a pig or an owl?

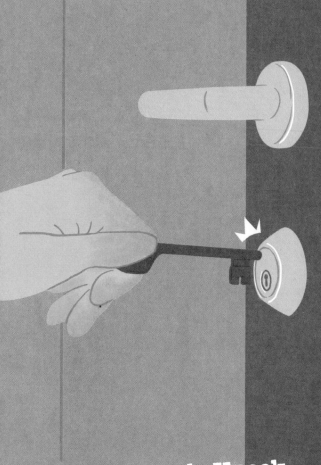

Knock Knock...
Who's there?
Doris
Doris who?
Doris locked, so I knocked!

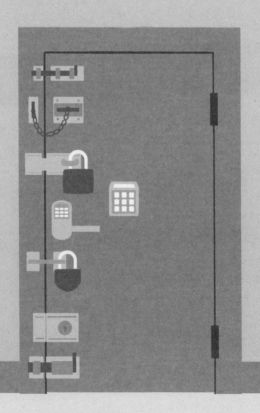

Knock Knock...
Who's there?
I.O
I.O who?
You owe me, when are you paying?

Knock Knock...
who's there?
Goat
Goat who?
Goat to the door and find out!

Knock Knock...
Who's there?
Pea catch
Pea catch who?
I choose you!

Knock Knock...
Who's there?
Viper
Viper who?
Viper nose, it's running!

Knock Knock...
Who's there?
Vindal
Vindal who?
Dinner's here!

Knock Knock...
Who's there?
Lettuce
Lettuce who?
Lettuce in, it's cold out here!

Knock Knock...
Who's there?
Interrupting sloth
Interrupting sloth who?
...
SLOOOOOTH!

Knock Knock...
who's there?
A pile up
A pile up who?
Ewww!

Knock Knock...
Who's there?
Cliffhanger
Cliffhanger who?
Find out next episode!

Knock Knock...
Who's there?
Maida
Maida who?
Maida force be with you!

Knock Knock...
Who's there?
Dunnop
Dunnop who?
Eww you've done a poo!

Knock Knock...

Who's there?

Toodle

Toodle who?

But I only just got here!

Knock Knock...
Who's there?
Joe
Joe who?
Joe King!

Knock Knock...
Who's there?
Imap
Imap who?
Yes you are!

Knock Knock...
Who's there?
Hope
Hope who?
Hope who like my jokes!

Knock Knock...
who's there?
Peeka
Peeka who?
I see you!

Knock Knock...
Who's there?
Wool
Wool who?
Wool who open this door already!

MOO!
Knock Knock...
who's there?
Time travelling cow
Time travelling cow who?

Knock Knock...
who's there?
Weevil
Weevil who?
**Weevil rock
you!**

Knock Knock...
Who's there?
Dora
Dora who?
Dora needs unlocking!

Knock Knock...
who's there?
Snow
Snow who?
Snow use, I've forgotten my name again!

Knock Knock...
Who's there?
Barbik
Barbik who?
You bring the burgers and I'll bring the sauce!

Knock Knock...
Who's there?
Nuisance
Nuisance who?
What's nuisance yesterday?

Knock Knock...

Who's there?

Eyesore

Eyesore who?

Eyesore do love you!

Knock Knock...
who's there?
Urchin
urchin who?
Urchin is rather pointy!

Knock Knock...
Who's there?
Doughnut
Doughnut who?
Doughnut who I was expecting!

Knock Knock...
Who's there?
Yah
Yah who?
Settle down, cowboy!

Knock Knock...
Who's there?
Interrupting dyslexic cow
Interrupting dysle...
OMO!